A Trunkful of Elephants

For Tracey and Neil, with love

A Trunkful of Elephants

Compiled by Judith Nicholls

Illustrated by Chris Riddell

MAMMOTH

This anthology comes with thanks to Adrienne Jones
and Emma Wakefield and film crew, poets Grace
Nichols and Paul Cookson, Brian Harman, and London
Zoo – and of course, Dilberta.

The idea for this book came from two excellent days
we shared filming with the elephants for *Middle English*.

Judith Nicholls

First published in Great Britain 1994
by Methuen Children's Books Ltd and Mammoth
imprints of Reed Consumer Books Ltd
Michelin House, 81 Fulham Road, London SW3 6RB
and Auckland, Melbourne, Singapore and Toronto

Copyright for this anthology © 1994 Judith Nicholls
Illustrations copyright © 1994 Chris Riddell

ISBN 0 7497 1753 X

A CIP catalogue record for this title
is available from the British Library

Printed in Great Britain by
BPC Paperbacks Ltd
A member of
The British Printing Company Ltd

Contents

IV *I WAS RAJAH*

V *ONCE THERE WAS AN ELEPHANT*

VI *I Dreamed a Dream*

I

A Kind of Wisdom

Postcard from Kinshasa

You will have forgotten this.

You sent
a postcard from Kinshasa.

A cow elephant charges the camera,
ivory like parentheses round that flailing trunk,
ears in the wind like army blankets.

You will have forgotten this
as I have nearly forgotten you.

But neither will forget the elephant,
tusks goring the air

FRED SEDGWICK

Evidence of Elephants

If you had had just the bones to go on,
  Only the bones,
Could you have guessed an elephant?
  How could you know?

Oh, you could work out the size and so on
  By measuring the bones,
But the vast flapping ears, that caked-mud grey,
  They would not show.

Nor the trunk. From the skull you'd never guess
  At that long swinging trunk,
Boneless and flexible, sensitive and beautiful,
  Hanging in front,

Or lifted to blare like a trumpet, or to caress
  Another elephant.
If I had only the bones to help me,
  I think I'd be stumped.

GERARD BENSON

The Blind Men and the Elephant

It was six men of Hindostan,
To learning much inclined,
Who went to see the elephant,
(Though all of them were blind):
That each by observation
Might satisfy his mind.

The *first* approached the Elephant,
And happening to fall
Against his broad and sturdy side,
At once began to bawl:
'Bless me, it seems the Elephant
Is very like a wall.'

The *second*, feeling of his tusk,
Cried, 'Ho! what have we here
So very round and smooth and sharp?
To me 'tis mighty clear
This wonder of an Elephant
Is very like a spear.'

The *third* approached the animal,
And happening to take
The squirming trunk within his hands,
Then boldly up and spake:
'I see,' quoth he, 'the Elephant
Is very like a snake.'

The *fourth* stretched out his eager hand
And felt about the knee,
'What most this mighty beast is like
Is mighty plain,' quoth he;
''Tis clear enough the Elephant
Is very like a tree.'

The *fifth* who chanced to touch the ear
Said, 'Even the blindest man
Can tell what this resembles most;
Deny the fact who can,
This marvel of an Elephant
Is very like a fan.'

The *sixth* no sooner had begun
About the beast to grope,
Than, seizing the swinging tail
That fell within his scope,
'I see,' cried he, 'the Elephant
Is very like a rope.'

And so these men of Hindostan
Disputed loud and long,
Each in his own opinion
Exceeding stiff and strong,
Though *each* was *partly* in the right
And all were in the wrong.

JOHN GODFREY SAXE

Nomad

A blousy tent
on a slow-go trail

A leathery balloon
swaying jungle-free

A sail-eared face
playing cascades

A house on stilts
trimming waves of air

KATHERINE GALLAGHER

Elephants Plodding

Plod! Plod!
And what ages of time
the worn arches of their spines support!

D. H. LAWRENCE

The Sentry

I like the way he moves,
his solemn purpose.
I like his feet,
gigantic pudding plates
that leave round blots
behind him on his journeys.
I like the curve his ears make
as he waits, quietly, there,
and on the far horizon
stands like a faithful sentry.

If I see
a kind of wisdom
that he carries with him,
thats how an elephant appears
to me.

JEAN KENWARD

The Elephant

Elephant, who brings death.
Elephant, a spirit in the bush.
With a single hand
He can pull two palm trees to the ground.
If he had two hands
He would tear the sky like an old rag.
The spirit who eats dog,
The spirit who eats ram,
The spirit who eats
A whole palm fruit with its thorns.
With his four mortar legs
He tramples down the grass.
Wherever he walks
The grass is forbidden to stand up again.

YORUBA PEOPLE, AFRICA

II

Thinking Big

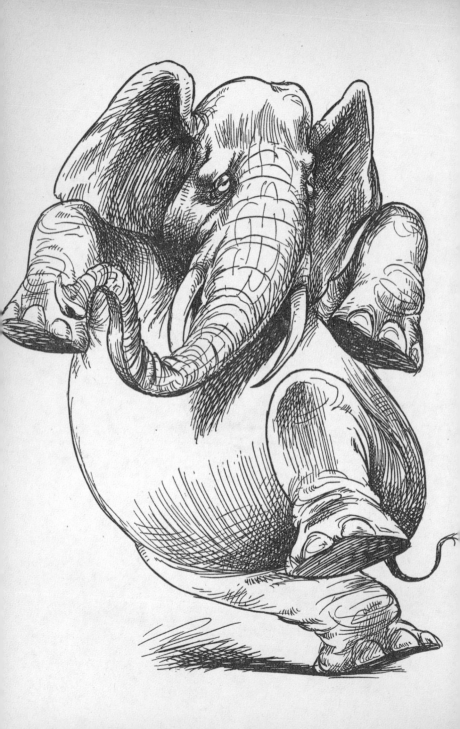

Elephant

It is quite unfair to be
obliged to be so large, so I suppose
you could call me discontented.

Think big, they said, when
I was a little elephant; they
wanted to get me used to it.

It was kind. But it doesn't help if,
inside, you are carefree in small ways,
fond of little amusements.

You are smaller than me, think
how conveniently near the flowers are,
how you can pat the cat by just

halfbending over. You can also
arrange teacups for dolls, play
marbles in the proper season.

I would give anything to be
able to do a tiny, airy, flitting
dance to show how very little a

thing happiness can be really.

ALAN BROWNJOHN

Relatives

'You are big!' said the little grey pachyderm,
 As he looked up his trunk at his mum.
'You are right!' And she smiled at the wit of her child
'I am certainly bigger than some!'

'You are small!' said the very big pachyderm,
 As she looked down her trunk, 'Child of mine,
 I think you should know: time will pass, you will grow,
 And become truly elephantine.'

IAN LARMONT

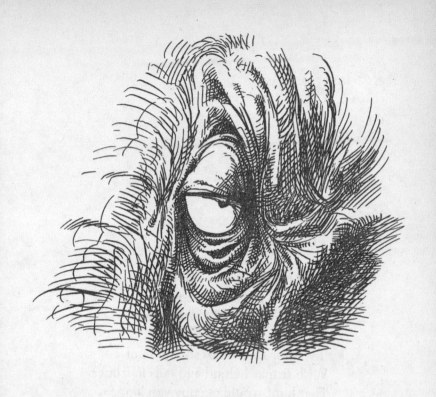

Pachyderm

Pachys: Greek for very thick,
And *derma*: Greek for skin,
Which helps to keep the weather out
And keep his insides in.

IAN LARMONT

25

The Force of Habit

A tail behind, a trunk in front,
Complete the usual elephant.
The tail in front, the trunk behind,
Is what you very seldom find.
If you for specimens should hunt
With trunks behind and tails in front
That hunt would occupy you long;
The force of habit is so strong.

A. E. HOUSMAN

The Elephant

When people call this beast to mind,
They marvel more and more
At such a LITTLE tail behind,
So LARGE a trunk before.

HILAIRE BELLOC

An Elephant's Nose Is Long I Suppose

An elephant's nose is long I suppose
to reach from her head to the tip of her toes
like an eye that smells out friends and foes
she uses it to say her hellos
hoover-like she sucks and blows
dust and sand she throws and throws
left and right and highs and lows
all of which just goes and shows
that an elephant knows how to use her nose.

PAUL COOKSON

Squirt!

What can an elephant
do with a trunk
when the sun is blazing hot?

He can
take it for a walk
to the waterhole,
suck a little water up
to make him cool –
then squirt all over his back,

THAT'S WHAT!
When the sun is blazing hot?

OH YES,
he can squirt all over his back!

WHY NOT?

JUDITH NICHOLLS

Funk

It may be the slap of his ears, my dear,
Or it may be the swipe of his trunk,
Or it may be the deadly bare bones of his tusks
That bring on the Elephant Funk –
For he'll only drink mud, mud, mud, you know,
Turns to jelly near pools that are clear,
Where his colly-w-wobbling reflection lurks
to *gobble him up*, my dear!

GINA WILSON

*'Elephants . . . drinke . . . water at all times,
whereof they will not tast, except it be muddy
and not cleare, for they avoid cleare water,
loathing to see their owne shaddow therein.'*

*from Historie of Four-footed Beastes (1607)
– Edward Topsell*

III

I Will Remember

PLEASE DO NOT
FEED

The Trunk

Above crisp packets,
Cans of Coke, and ice-creams,
using a finger with sixty
Thousand muscles, a mountain seems

To be looking for something;
Not just for twig ends,
The soft bark of young trees,
And the salt-lick that sends

Minerals to feed its mind,
But something beyond the sea
Of faces, the jungle
Of towerblocks; that we

Can't throw over a wall
Or through gaps in a cage,
Because this isn't a finger
Like ours that searches a page,

Or a vacuum cleaner
That sucks up any old junk:
This is an elephant looking
For Africa with its trunk.

JOHN LYNCH

Toomai of the Elephants

I will remember what I was. I am sick of rope and chain.
I will remember my old strength and all my forest affairs.
I will not sell my back to man for a bundle of sugar-cane,
I will go out to my own kind, and the wood-folk in their lairs.

I will go out until the day, until the morning break,
Out to the winds' untainted kiss, the waters' clean caress:
I will forget my ankle-ring and snap my picket-stake.
I will revisit my lost loves, and playmates masterless!

RUDYARD KIPLING

For Dilberta
(Biggest of the elephants at London Zoo)

The walking-whale
of the earth kingdom – Dilberta.

The one whose waist
our arms won't get around – Dilberta.

The mammoth one whose weight
you pray, won't knock you to the ground.

The one who displays toes
like archway windows,
bringing the pads of her feet down
like giant paperweights
to keep the earth from shifting about.

Dilberta, rippling as she ambles under
the wrinkled tarpaulin of her skin,
casually throwing the arm of her nose,
saying, 'Go on, have a stroke.'

But sometimes, in her mind's eye,
Dilberta gets this idea – she could be a moth!
Yes with the wind stirring behind her ears,
she could really fly.

Rising above the boundaries of the paddock,
Making for the dark light of the forest –

Hearing, O once more, the trumpets roar.

GRACE NICHOLS

Elegy

'Mummy, what was an elephant?'

Each ear was tuned to the forest,
each trunk uncurled to the sun;
each forehead domed against a sky
unchanged since time began.

Each head was raised in greeting
as they swayed from each new dawn,
and the timeless paths of the forest
echoed with trumpet-song.

Now the skies are dark,
the paths have gone;
what once was a forest
has turned to stone.
Now only vultures
shadow the sky
and the queens of the forest
are left, to die.

Before we are silenced,
hear our song;
before we are silenced,
hear our cry.

JUDITH NICHOLLS

Meditation in a Brighton Junkshop

This great, grey Emperor who moved and swayed
Like a procession to an unseen brass band
Was slaughtered, and his giant's foot sawn off
To make some idiot this umbrella-stand.

RAYMOND WILSON

Good Taste

The vilest furniture in this land
is an elephant's foot umbrella stand.

ADRIAN MITCHELL

Elephant Proverb

A man in his house
Breeds the peace we need.
But man in our bush
Carries death and greed.

DAVID POULTER

from *The Progresse of the Soule*

Nature's great masterpiece, an elephant
(The only harmless great thing), the giant
Of beasts, who thought none had to make him wise,
But to be just and thankful, loth to offend
(Yet nature hath given him no knees to bend)
Himself he up-props, on himself relies,
And, foe to none, suspects no enemies.

JOHN DONNE

The Elephant Table

Grandma boot-polished them
    glistening black –
four mahogany heads
facing north, south, east, west
    with a world on their back,

a world carved out whole
    from one slice of a tree,
a world that grew old
while the Viceroy asked princes
    to treaties and tea

and outside in the dust
    quiet lean watchful men
and their elephants waited
what seemed like an age
    for the party to end.

In Grandma's dark parlour
     I crouched eye to eye
with the south-facing elephant.
Where was it looking
     so weary, and why?

And what makes me reach back
     years later to feel
little-finger-sized tusks?
'Those are precious,' said Grandma.
     'They're real.'

PHILIP GROSS

Future Past

Lord of Africa,
swaying giant of the plains;
tree-mover,
sand-tosser,
diviner of water
from the dry river bed:
where are you now?

Where is the song on ivory keys
that echoed through the dusk?
The song's cut away
for a handful of beads
which once were a living tusk.
Now only baubles
glint in the sun,
for the forest lord fell
to the sound of a gun.

JUDITH NICHOLLS

If Only Elephants

If elephants were Man's Best Friend
and slept in wicker baskets by the fire,
ate supermarket forest
cooked and canned,
came when we called,
wore fur we could admire,
we wouldn't see them massacred for tusks.

We'd paint their toenails,
show them off at Crufts.

IRENE RAWNSLEY

Moon Forest

In the hush of a moon forest,
Knee bent, with toes spread hard
On a milk and golden orchid
Flowered from the fallen tree,
The elephant stopped –
Still free, still free!

His glistened ears swung out,
Listened to hill past hill
Voices of the far grasslands
Whispered from spear to spear,
Mysteriously near –
Beware, beware!

ANNABEL FARJEON

Elephants in the Circus

Elephants in the circus
have aeons of weariness round their eyes.
Yet they sit up
and show vast bellies to the children.

D. H. LAWRENCE

Captive Creature

Elephant restless in circus, in zoo,
pacing and pawing at concrete and bar,
longing for freedom and wide-open spaces,
leading processions, bedecked with *howdah*,
drooping with feathers and wearing a tutu,
learning, on two legs, to balance and dance.
Juggling with balls. Being put through such paces
doesn't give dignity much of a chance.

GINA DOUTHWAITE

Circus Elephant

Does the Elephant remember
In the grey light before dawn,
Old noises of the jungle
In mornings long gone?

Does the Elephant remember
The cry of hungry beasts,
The Tiger and the Leopard,
The Lion at his feasts?

Do his mighty eardrums listen
For the thunder of the feet
Of the Buffalo and the Zebra
In the dark and dreadful heat?

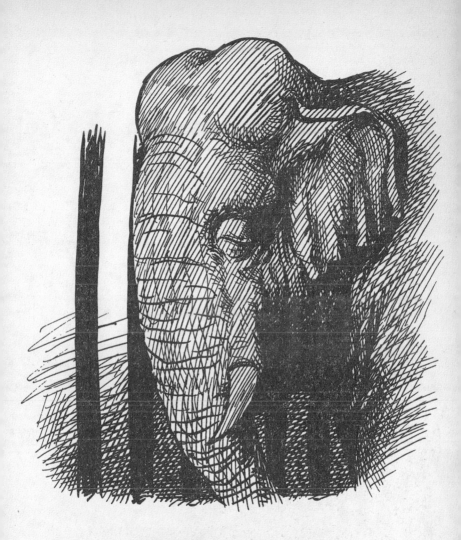

Does His Majesty remember,
Does he stir himself and dream
Of the long-forgotten music
Of a long-forgotten dream?

KATHRYN WORTH

IV

I Was Rajah

Dressed for War

Dressed for war.
Patient, placid soul.
Tusks shod in steel,
Trained to charge and gore.
Dressed for war.

Dressed for war.
Victory the goal.
Pain from anvil'd steel,
Spearpoint to the jaw.
Dressed for war.

Dressed for war.
Weapons take their toll,
Eyes pierced by steel,
What's the suffering for?
Dressed and done for . . . war.

IAN LARMONT

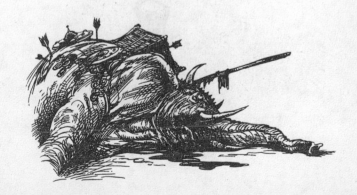

An Elephant Remembers

I was Rajah
Emperor of all elephants,
On the feasts of Dasera and Diwali
I was clothed like a king
In sumptuous trappings
Of gold and silver brocade.
My howdah was covered with silk,
Blue as the royal peacock,
Beautiful girls rode on my back,
Their black hair fragrant
with frangipani blossoms,
Their laughter bright as temple bells.
How majestically I swayed
Through streets seething with people,
The scent of sandalwood and jasmine,
Cardamom and cumin,
The riot of morning glory flowers
And the hot dust.

I am old now
And stiff in my bones,
But I can still feel
The soft touch of a sari,
Turn my head to the chime
Of bell and gong.

THERESA HEINE

Hannibal's Elephants —
a terrified scout reports

They're coming over the mountains,
the creatures made of stone.
There's nothing can resist them
that's made of flesh and bone.

They set the rocks a-tremble.
They cause the earth to quake.
Each leg is like a tree-trunk.
Each nose is like a snake.

Each back is like a boulder.
Each head high as a hill.
They shake the dead with every tread.
Their cry is wild and shrill.

They're coming over the mountains.
How can such beasts be real?
Whoever stands to fight with them
must have a heart of steel.

They're coming over the mountains,
these creatures made of stone.
How can we hope to hold them back
with flesh and blood and bone?

TONY MITTON

Note: In 218 BC the Carthaginian general, Hannibal, led his army and its war elephants across the Alps into Italy, where he defeated the Roman legions three times over.

Elephant Dreams

1 I'm so small
   I can crawl
   under a leaf

   and I can look
   into the world
   from underneath.

2 There's a huge grey cloud in the sky.
   It's me.
   I float down on to a sycamore
   tree.
   I burst like a bag and the rain falls
   out.
   I swim in my rain like a huge grey
   trout.

3 My
   long
   trunk
   goes
   round
   the
   world
   twice!

4   I am the last elephant
and I stare into the sun
as it falls into the night
and in the fading light
I know my race is run.
I am the last elephant.

5   I can't move.
People are staring at me.

I can't move.
People are walking by.

I can't move.
Children are pointing at me.

I can't move.
Is this where you go when you die?

IAN McMILLAN

White Elephants

In Thailand many years ago
When people called the place Siam,
It was the King who ran the show
And did just what he wanted to.
  He was the great *I am*!

The King claimed as his lawful right
Albino elephants – that is,
All elephants whose colour might
Be said to approximate to white.
  He claimed they *all* were *his*.

Elephants then were in demand
And worked to keep the economy healthy –
They were the cranes, the lorries and
Bulldozers that throughout the land
  Kept their possessors wealthy.

White elephants were quite different,
For they were sacred, like the King,
And therefore could not work, which meant
They led lives that were indolent
  And never did a thing.

The cost of feeding them, alas,
Was ruinous and frightful,
And so the King, it came to pass,
Used them as sly gifts when he was
  Determined to be spiteful.

White elephants were presents that
Were worse than useless to their masters.
Remember this when next you're at
A jumble sale. Take care the things
  You're buying aren't disasters!

RAYMOND WILSON

V

Once There Was an Elephant

Elephantasy

'There's been an elephant in my fridge,'
 I heard an old man mutter.
'How can you tell?' I asked him –
 'Footprints in the butter!'

'The elephant's still in there.'
 The old man gave a 'Tut!'
'How do you know?' I asked him –
 'Look, the door won't shut!'

CELIA WARREN

The Elephant's Dictionary

Elegant:
What elephants always are
Especially at dinner.

Elevator:
How elephants go upstairs.

Elocution:
Polite trumpetings.

Elicopter:
Used by the elephant Flying Squad.

Elevision:
Home entertainment for the elephant
(also known as ellytelly).

Elescope:
A long-sighted elephant.

Elepathic:
A far-sighted elephant.

Elephone:
For trunk calls.

Elementary:
Infants' school for tiny tuskers.

Elegy:
Sad elephant's song.

Elements:
Rough weather for crossing the Alps.

Eletosis:
Bad breath on an elephant's tongue.

Elligator:
A snappy dresser amongst the pachyderms.

DAVID HARMER

Elephantasia

If an elephant wore big rubber boots –
Would it be a Wellyphant?

Or if one was raspberry red and wobbly –
Could it be a Jellyphant?

If you saw one on a TV show –
Might it be a Telephant?

What if an elephant never had a shower –
Would he be a Smellyphant?

Or if one got so very, very fat –
Might we say Pot-bellyphant?

Do you think we'll ever, ever know?

No, not on your Nelly-phant!

DAVID WHITEHEAD

Eletelephony

Once there was an elephant,
Who tried to use the telephant –
No! No! I mean an elephone
Who tried to use the telephone –
(Dear me! I am not certain quite
That even now I've got it right.)

Howe'er it was, he got his trunk
Entangled in the telephunk;
The more he tried to get it free
The louder buzzed the telephee –
(I fear I'd better drop the song
of elephop and telephong!)

LAURA E. RICHARDS

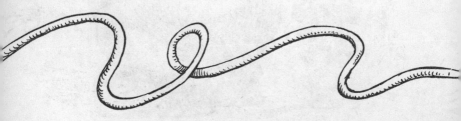

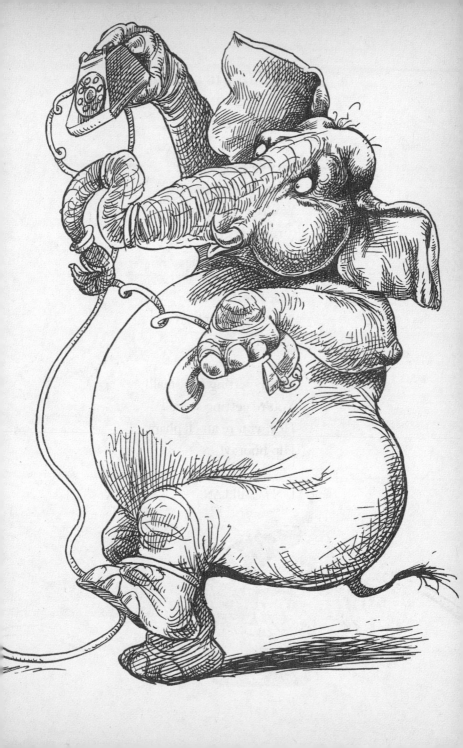

Spell to Turn Your Brother or Sister into an Elephant

Ears getting bigger!
Nose getting longer!
You're getting taller,
turning grey!

Teeth getting tusky!
Voice getting rusty!
You're getting heavy,
turning grey!

Room getting too small!
You're getting so tall!
Hey, you're an elephant!
Hip hooray!

IAN McMILLAN

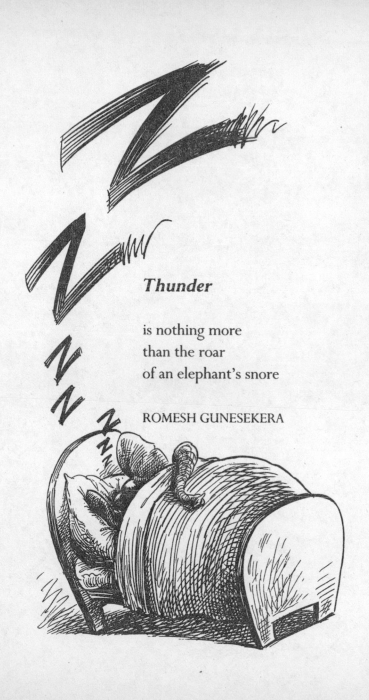

Thunder

is nothing more
than the roar
of an elephant's snore

ROMESH GUNESEKERA

VI

I Dreamed a Dream

A Dream of Elephants

I dreamed a dream of elephants.
I cannot tell you why.
But in my dream I saw the herd
go slowly walking by.

They moved beneath a blazing sun,
through rising dust and heat.
They made their solemn journey
on strong and silent feet.

And in my dream I heard a voice.
But why, I do not know.
It whispered, 'Where is there a place
that such as these may go?'

Then as I watched, the solemn herd
walked slowly, sadly by,
until I stood, amazed, alone,
beneath a silent sky.

I watched them as they moved away.
I watched as they walked on.
They merged into the heat and dust
till all of them were gone.

I dreamed a dream of elephants.
I cannot tell you why.
But in my dream I saw the herd
go slowly walking by.

TONY MITTON

Elephants

(for Erica who collects them)

Temples built to meditate
Upon themselves are elephants
Whose pillars bear the cloudy weight
Of some remote intelligence
Which hesitates, which shyly comes
To bless us all, then disappears
Though offered penitential buns
By kids who wash behind their ears.

JOHN MOLE

Two Small Boys and an Elephant

That was hopeless love, when the brothers gazed
at elephants at the Zoo.

One turned great grey legs and back on them
as elephants do.

Brothers gazed after elephant with love
and then, on cue,

returned to loving ice creams
as small boys do.

FRED SEDGWICK

Turn Turn Turn

There is a time for considering elephants
There is no time for not considering elephants

ADRIAN MITCHELL

ACKNOWLEDGEMENTS

'The Elephant' by Hilaire Belloc, copyright © The Estate of Hilaire Belloc 1970, reprinted by permission of the Peters Fraser & Dunlop Group Ltd.

'Evidence of Elephants' by Gerard Benson, copyright © Gerard Benson 1994.

'Elephant' by Alan Brownjohn from *Brownjohn's Beasts*, published by Macmillan 1970, copyright © Alan Brownjohn 1970.

'An Elephant's Nose Is Long I Suppose' by Paul Cookson, copyright © Paul Cookson 1994.

'Captive Creature' by Gina Douthwaite, copyright © Gina Douthwaite 1994.

'Moon Forest' by Annabel Farjeon, copyright © Annabel Farjeon 1994.

'Nomad' by Katherine Gallagher, copyright © Katherine Gallagher 1994.

'The Elephant Table' by Philip Gross, copyright © Philip Gross 1994.

'Thunder' by Romesh Gunesekera, copyright © Romesh Gunesekera 1991.

'The Elephant's Dictionary' by David Harmer, copyright © David Harmer 1994.

A selected list of titles available from Mammoth

☐	7497 0095 5	**Among Friends**	Caroline B Cooney £2.99
☐	7497 0145 5	**Through the Nightsea Wall**	Otto Coontz £2.99
☐	7497 0582 5	**The Promise**	Monica Hughes £2.99
☐	7497 0171 4	**One Step Beyond**	Pete Johnson £2.50
☐	7497 0281 8	**The Homeward Bounders**	Diana Wynne Jones £2.99
☐	7497 0312 1	**The Changeover**	Margaret Mahy £2.99
☐	7497 0473 X	**Shellshock**	Anthony Masters £2.99
☐	7497 0323 7	**Silver**	Norma Fox Mazer £3.50
☐	7497 0325 3	**The Girl of his Dreams**	Harry Mazer £2.99
☐	7497 0280 X	**Beyond the Labyrinth**	Gillian Rubinstein £2.50
☐	7497 0558 2	**Frankie's Story**	Catherine Sefton £2.50
☐	7497 0009 2	**Secret Diary of Adrian Mole**	Sue Townsend £2.99
☐	7497 0333 4	**Plague 99**	Jean Ure £2.99
☐	7497 0147 1	**A Walk on the Wild Side**	Robert Westall £2.99